THE CARNIVOROUS GAZE

To Walker,
whose name is a poem.

All the best,

Sue Parman

Colrain Poetry Conference
September 2015

To J., my meat and drink

Sue Parman is Professor Emeritus of Anthropology, as
well as an award-winning poet, playwright, fiction
writer, and artist. Her chapbook *The Thin Monster
House* was published by Finishing Line Press in
2012. See http://anthro.fullerton.edu/sparman/ and
www.sueparman.com.

The following poems first appeared in these journals:
"Body Parts" and "Balter" (*Fault Lines*), "Emily
Dickinson's Dog" (*The Blue Mouse*), "Finifugal"
(*Verseweavers*), "What Will I Do When I'm Dead"
(*Bewildering Stories*), "Oregon" (*Concord*).

Yond' Cassius has a lean and hungry look;
He thinks too much: such men are dangerous.
Shakespeare, *Julius Caesar*

Contents

I.

II.

III.

IV.

V.

The Carnivorous Gaze

They say hunger's internal,
self-referential, some infernal
wreckage of self-control.
But I never knew
hunger until you (that otherness,
the not-me and never-wasness)
rose up like a garden of odd vegetables
that I stir-fried instead of the old
bake or double-bubble, and the vowels
clung to new consonants, the smell of which
turned me carnivorous. I learned
there was meat on the bones of the world,
and to eat was to burn. Who knew?
You think I'm dangerous?
Come closer and I'll show you.

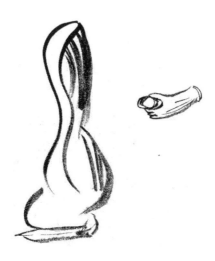

Monsters

Mine are thin monsters,
the kind that slither between the cracks
of acceptable lives, of stable times;
the monsters that poke their heads up
to check on the work in progress
that is a life or pretends to be;
the monsters that root around in unstable DNA
and tip the C's toward A's, the G's toward T's,
not the grizzly kind that rips up beds,
the bee swarm that sends lemmings over cliffs
but the kind that lingers, causing gasps
in the middle of mid-day naps;
the would-have, could-be, would-be ifs
that make our losses more, our triumphs less.

That's why this is a stumbling double septet.
It's hard to craft a memoir from regret.

She's Such

She's such a—well, you know.
The kind of girl who—it's hard to say.
Like a shadow really. Doesn't ever commit.
Leaves before the end. How does she get home?
She's one of those mountain brats,
father an engineer or something like that.
Maybe she doesn't have a mother—
that's likely, given those clothes.
They say she writes.
Oh, one of those.

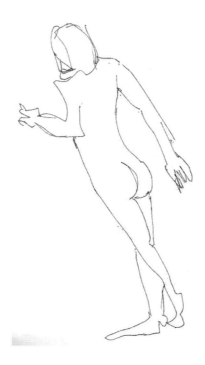

Stubborn

Stubborn is that first attempt to tie a shoe lace:
uneven teeth fixed in a lip-drawn grimace,
crimp-cramp skinny fingerbones braced
against rough leather. Quit, relax, try again
some other time. No! Can't let it go,

push past the sense of it all, there's rain
outside anyway, no walk today. That's not
the point. Fine, have it your own way,
walks away, even brings out the peanut butter,
but for now there is no other form of play

on the table. Again and again, pinch strings
together, push them under each other,
what a haphazard, arbitrary way of tightening
the edges of the universe. Pull hard.
It's all my fault if the world comes loose.

It's not being stubborn, really, just following
a path the feet stepped into. Going this way,
why not? The relief of action in a world
of uncertainty. Choose, it doesn't matter
which path. The very fact of walking keeps us

upright. It's the forward momentum, the joy
of discovering direction. For want of a shoelace
a life drizzled to a halt and the numbness began.
Stubborn: unhook the fingers, plunge them in
to this, to that, to anything.

History Lesson

I never think of you as wearing clothes
you put on, take off. You are always
fully dressed, like a knight in armor,
a mannequin of the high school supermarket,
a teacher of Western Civ
who teaches us how ancient people live
and grade our papers and make us think
(smearing the words of my essay is a round
brown stain, a coffee cup set down--
I imagine the taste of my words in your drink)
until one day you say that medieval people
never bathed, never changed their clothes.
There is a hot stillness in the room.
The sun catches your high forehead, parts your
thinning hair,
lights up the buttons you undo—
a sports jacket, the one you always wear.
You slide off the jacket and I suddenly smell the rot
of accumulated undergarments falling off,
the taste of unwashed hair and skin,
the hint of unshaved hair beneath the chin.
And suddenly your words catch fire
in the space where the short sleeves and the wrist
bones meet:
a zone of history, a syllabus of desire
transcribed on your arm so bare,
so indiscreet.

Dead Cat Stories

Gayle tells stories about her dead cats: how they never
had much luck. Like the Siberian Shorthair
that was hungry and jumped into the freezer,
or the Russian Blue attracted to truckers,
last seen in the well of an eighteen-wheeler.

The worst death was the little black cat
that only Gayle liked. Last seen on the back
porch, someone had tied its tail to a kite.
All they found were the eyeballs, fried
from the lightning strikes. "All my poor dead cats,"

      she says. "I had five when I lived at home."
      Her mother insists she had only one.

Rapunzel

There are two main questions here:
the tower and the hair.
Which is less likely: that a girl is raised from infant
to teenager
at the top of a closed tower without an elevator
so the evil witch has to climb those seventeen
hundred stairs
to deliver the pabulum or peanut butter,
to bring up the dresses and underwear;
or that a girl without exercise or fresh air
somehow manages to grow 20-foot-long hair?
Did she practice yoga for hair follicles?
Or was she so bored that she had
an out of the normal hair body miracle?

To My Father Who Asked Me,
When I was Four,
When is a Door Not a Door?

A door is always a door except when it's a jar
to take your offerings. You leave and your leavings
take you far.

A door has two sides, two states of being: ajar
or closed, arrived or leaving. On my way out
I left you this offering.

Is it Worth a Lot?

It took a while for my father to learn
that when he traveled he should bring home gifts.
He often forgot and never got the hang of it.
My mother was easy—Chanel #5. My sister
a glass horse. I got the weird stuff
as if he couldn't figure me out. One time
there was a postage stamp. "Put it under
the microscope," he said. I expected
rainbows or a lost world and got
the bible. Once a bundle of rawhide scraps.
And then there was the chunk of dirty glass
he revealed in his slowly opened hands.
"It's a diamond," he said. "Man-made."
"Is it worth a lot?" I asked. But he didn't speak,
as if not knowing what to say.

The Box

My box is small. I would like to throw out
the Technicolor imagery and leave only the smells
(the bruised juniper of my parents' double martinis,
the amaretto my father snuck into the meatloaf
despite my mother's distrust of seasonings).
They say seeing is believing but don't believe it.
I'll trade you a hundred visions of a saint
for the smell of a carbonized Sunday roast.

Maybe there's something to be said for the red
wheelbarrow
and the blue guitar, but I'll leave them in someone
else's box.
I have my own allotments: what to throw out,
what adverbs do I exchange for one more noun
renowned for its contemplation and abstraction,
what heroes traded for zeros. I idolize subtraction,
strip away the plenitude; leave only the thirst.
It was from Shakespeare I learned how to curse.

My little dark box is almost empty now,
fumigated for its false positives, with a stinky
cheese
smell all its own. I left home a long time ago.
I was abstemious even then, yet cursed with
plenitude—
too many words, the places to put them few—
until it occurred to me to drop them in a box
and there they stayed, with the double martinis and
amaretto,
until I finally learned to say no.

Poems in my Mother's Kitchen

I see poems in my mother's shining kitchen,
in the apples she never trusted to cinnamon.
I see poems in the spice rack I gave her for
Christmas,
the empty plastic cylinders and their blank labels
staring down the espresso machine in its unopened
box.
There are poems in the empty sugar bowl
and the bagels without sour cream or lox,
and the green beans cooked without tarragon
in the pressure cooker. Fire's a hard master:
In the vinegar-clean kitchen it calls home,
it requires its own special poem.

Blue Moon

Blue shows up a lot in songs and poetry:
I sing the blues, I am blue, blue moon.
But not all blues are blue. They are spun
with the white of cerulean,
the green of turquoise, and the angry hue
of world-hungry vermillion.
Anything is better than the blue of cold sadness,
that woeful countenance of arctic ice
in a parent's judgmental eyes.
Get over memories of the dead.
Bring on the red.

Jean Simeon Chardin, Soap Bubbles

The Greeks equated life with breath,
like a soap bubble blown—
all fragile, thin-skin, iridescent
unlike the rosy flesh and thickened bone

that holds the straw and the pursed red lips
that blow—life-giving themselves and presumably
unsusceptible to death. But observe the tips
of the fingers: the darkening

seams of age, decay, and change,
the cheeks flushed and feverish, the brow
pulsing with effort and the sleeve with its strange
flounce like stuffing coming out.

If life is breath then like the skin
of the iridescent bubble we grow thin
and with an excess of breath expire,
exploded by a puff of fire—

or simply flatten and evaporate.
All lines go down. The cosign
of my father's calculus is flat:
the skin, the energy, the lively mind

all tend toward horizontal. He still
has peaks, but mostly this aging sire
tends toward slow sleep, his attention
a leaf drifting over a dying fire.

Death moves in him like ice on a flowing river,
a thick-chunk denseness, opaque.
His bones solidify and quiver,
shutting down. Blue eyes turn gray.

Through all the symptoms of death I notice
his fingernails: unbroken keratin,
no cloudy half-moons,
the flush of good circulation.

He will not die from hangnail or gangrene.
The death that grows is somewhere deep inside—
in his heart, in the cavity of his mind,
in his sad soap bubble spirit wandering,

And when he dies and goes fully horizontal,
his fingernails will glow with health
and go on without him, wherever he is,
his windowless, fingerless self.

Fire and Ice

My father died like a fire
in embers, burned down
to the last hard cinders.
I don't think he died
lonely. He had settled in
like a bear in his den
to sleep for the winter of his life,
surrounded by ice.

We make our dens in the wilderness
with strangers to keep off the wolves,
a final fire at our feet and head.
And in the end it only matters
that we have a bed, a kind of home,
a den, protection as we sleep,
as life slides off the bone.

He didn't suffer, the nurse said.
He kept quoting T.S. Eliot.
He went to sleep and never woke up.
The fact is he went to sleep
a long time ago, slipping from poem to hymn,
dying all his life
with gentle wolves to watch over him.

He died no bother to anyone,
With the words "I'm sorry" on his tongue.
Sorry for what? For bothering the nurse
with his poetry? For being dependent
on the kindness of paid strangers?
For the things not said or done,
not to mention those other things,

the betrayals and departures
that had little to do with final raptures?

His life was a leap from one den to another,
each with a different mother.
A partner, a wife—too much responsibility.
Daughters (not sons) a liability.
Things unfinished, a war unfought.
Life has a way of going on without
resolution. His constitution

was bear-like, solid, a rock
that sagged when leaned upon
but broke walls when he fell.
"You can tell," said the cabbalist
with his mystic symbols, "a Jew
by his nose." My Lutheran father knew
the symbols of cybernetics and the rose
but was frequently misled by frauds
and madmen, by their howl.
He was escorted home by an owl.

When women die, does the air whirl
in their wake? In the end
do owls attend and banners unfurl?
No, they usually go
unremarked by the incandescent air,
for theirs is the way of sin and error,
the invisible set in the tableware
of gods and wars and holy terror--
we small words, like "it" and "them"
who in our living let loose the deaths of men.

When I die, let me die in ice,
not melted into embered earth.
Let my pact with words suffice.

Golf:
Special Rules During the War
Richmond Golf Club, England, 1940

(For my Father, who Stopped Playing Golf only
When he went Blind, and who Gave my Golf Clubs
to my Cousin)

It goes without saying that golf's not a bore;
that you play it each day. Oh, how I abhor
      excuses like sickness
      or sleet-icy slickness
or, heaven forbid it, a war.

But in the event that a war intervenes
all golfers, whether single or playing in teams,
      may dive and take cover
      and no one will suffer
from penalties caused by the screams.

Delayed bombs are marked with a flag made of
teak,
without guarantees for the living or weak.
      If you play, keep in mind
      that delayed-action mines
can disrupt the most careful technique.

Please remove shrapnel from off of the green
to prevent any damage to mowing machines.
      If a ball is destroyed,
      don't delay—send a boy
to replace it before having tea.

A player who suffers from nerves might go broke
if he bets when a bomber delivers his load.
      He must suck in his gut,
         curse the war and his luck,
and accept the odd penalty stroke.

But a war must inevitably come to a stop,
and although all your parents and lovers are lost,
         don't you fret. Bend your knee.
      A worse thing would be
if you lost your enjoyment for golf.

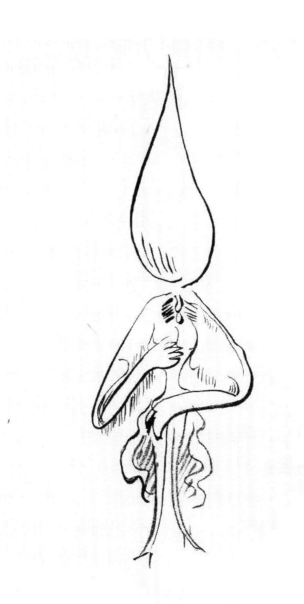

Scarlatina

I was sick the first year of the cold war.
Even my tongue was hot. It seared the ginger ale
and boiled the lime jello. I read Altscheler,
whose green Kentucky hills kept my head clear
as long as my eyes stayed on the page. My bed
floated on a creaking redwood floor
above the beginnings of the bomb shelter I had dug
when we first moved here, until my mother said
that radiation couldn't penetrate our books. I
expected
my skin to turn scarlet and peel off. They didn't tell
me
that if I read I might go blind. Which may explain
why my mother threw my books on the floor—the
books
I'd piled high around me. Why,
if atomic bombs peel the skin from your eyes,
do they call it a cold war? I fought back. I thought
she was taking away my talismans,
the only thing between me and annihilation.

Christmas Gift

A can of sardines, I thought,
unwrapping the ribboned tissue under the tree
(my father never used scotch tape so I always knew
which were his presents). So narrow,
so small, like his imagination,
a present bought at the last minute
(at least he remembered I told myself).
All the lights out except for the logs in the fireplace,
a warm burn in the always-cold house
(choose which side to freeze) and the small red
lights
of the plastic red chilies like stars in a distant sky
that suddenly moves inside,
spreading its dusky heart of poisoned gray
like mercury, the river on which I sail away
from home and all Christmases.
But I take my father's gift with me
and in a distant city in a stranger's place
open the can and find the rattlesnake.
I taste the color of the sky, its grit and broken
bones,
the gray heart of its suffering.
In the legend of the white snake
the hero speaks a thousand tongues.
But some languages can never be understood
no matter how many rattlesnakes you eat,
just as some skies will always be empty
and their colors numb.

Silence

I could sing like the wind-whistling women
on their porch swings, sour as green
crabapples on the stem, or a frog
in heat. I could hum
a twelve-tone strum on a blue guitar,
but that is not what is or how things are.

Things too terrible for words are mum.
They sear speech centers, take away
your tongue. The light around you
smells of green laundry and ozone,
and when you pick up the phone to call,
there isn't even a dial tone.

When asteroids hit earth,
the Martians might have looked on and said
Good, they deserved that, Look how they were
carrying on
with ferns and a waste of space, all that water.
It's all wrong, too many notes.
Give us purple wind and dust motes.

But here on earth, with the dinosaurs dying,
Martian gossip goes unheard. A disaster
is personal; more than the sum of its parts.
It's not science but art--
an inverted art that spirals in
on sunless, tongueless nothingness.

Oh bird of death that pecks out the eye
of the great white whale, you've cut my throat.
Let there be feathers in the bird cage,
let there be monsters in the park.
Let there be headless Hamlets on the stage.
Let there be silence in the dark.

The Patron Saint of Lost Causes

If I believed in saints and carried their icons
on a chain in the hollow of my throat
I would choose as my patron the one
who beats the bushes for lost causes.
We'll start small: like learning to make a bed,
wash out my coffee cup, clean the long hairs
from the vacuum cleaner. Answer letters,
fix the e on the typewriter, return phone calls,
sit where everyone else sits to get
attention. Wash your face
three times a day. Fold business letters
the right way. Stand up to salute the flag,
especially the God part. Mute your disbelief
to agnosticism. "I don't know" is safer,
boyfriend-wise, to laughter. It's lonely this way
but nice to know that a lot of time is saved
by the lack of signifying,
by not trying. You know the high cost
of denying something's lost.

Hebridean Love Song

I met a man while climbing sunwise
up a sheepflanked hill. He did not meet my eyes
but I saw his, and how he wept,
or was it rain, the mist of chaos-swept
and lonely history of sea-locked islands,
lochs and highland whispering
of seaweed and the sacrifice
of those who stay. He was

a man in stature bent like purple heather,
sear and firm, his essence salt
and granite, gray in color, rich in taste.
He would not look me in the face,
would not admit to taste or color.
Just a man, a hawk, a guardian of lambs,
who wraps himself at night in plaid and heather,
watched by birds, who shield him from the weather.

We paused. Our words were small, like dew,
or far-lit stars, or man. A curlew called,
a crew of grouse and raucous silences
hung damp, inebriated on the dew, sincere.
And of the spiral spectrum of the human sphere
no flame burned in his eyes, nor fear;
his face a mask upon a stony grave.
His speech sprang from some frozen plane

of grief-soaked secrets locked inside his brain,
occluded and obscure. I saw him
starling-marked with birdsong in his words
and star-crossed in his history of love,
a man who hid himself away with birds

and counted rhododendrons in the grove.
And though my touch in meeting met the bone
and frozen silence of a hermit wanderer,
yet I would ferry him across the turgid river
farther than a friendly lover—
frank and fond, as brother to another;
as if we came from the same death,
a similar mother.

I Never Thought You
Would Think of Me

I never thought you would think of me
as someone other than what I thought I was.
But when you came for that first visit
four years before you died, it occurred to me
you might have thought I was—well,
rich, or part of a different community.
We had known each other for thirty years by then.
It was your first visit—part of your quest to pursue
Stevenson (I have the books you brought,
your introduction to the latest edition of *Kidnapped*
reminding me of my father's careful syntax;
your pledge of friendship indelible). What did you
think, I asked when you called to say
you'd made it home. "It bears much thinking,"
you said. Then silence, a long pause,
during which it occurred to me
you had never thought to wonder who I was.

The Gathering Together Farm
on Route 20

In half a mile is the Gathering Together Farm
not to be confused with the Gathering Apart Farm
that lies at the end of Xeno's Road
(you know, the road that you never reach the end of
on account of the paradox). And some distance
after that
is the Gathering of the Eternally Split Up but
Nevertheless Hopeful Farm
where no one lives because the map drops off
and only the dead know the address.

Hard Love

When I'm constipated I think of you:
A consternation of the guts.
I was relieved when we were through.

I struggled with the bland diet of your silence.
You had difficulty digesting my words
(Too much fiber, too dense).

Like a difficult shit,
you left memories of your passing.
I made you thick.

Digesting love is what I miss most.
But sometimes instead of oatmeal grains,
it's cellulose.

To wit, to woo:
If you were hard on me, my love,
what was I to you?

Don't wait around. Get off the pot,
find another love,
take an enema and sleep well,

knowing life will go on without me.
The peristalsis of our love
was slow and virtuous, as dull

as chaff, as unsustaining. In a word,
you sucked out all the liquids, leaving
in the end, a turd.

Body Parts

Lovers praise their loved ones' cheek and nose,
their swanlike neck and gentle brow,
the rubies of their lips, the silver glow
within the orbit of the eye. Yet who knows
the body parts that are ignored?
There are names not only for things
like lip and eye and chin
but for the spaces in between.
How do we find them? You aim for a kiss and slip,
and hit the philtrum just above the upper lip
(the "love cup" where the sap of love is sipped)
or the supra-sternal notch below the throat.
Too close to focus on the eyes, you choose
to kiss the space between the eyebrows and the nose
(glabella, from the word for "smooth").
There's nothing like an accident
to shipwreck us in things we take for granted.

Marriage Agreement

A marriage is based solely on agreement:
If she agrees to vacuum the carpets
he agrees to polish the floor.
If she tells white lies to his mother,
he backs her up. The same goes
for children: create a façade
of clear yesses and no's,
of deadlines for the prom and when
homework must be done.
As the years go on,
the agreements get shaped
to lives as they are lived:
He strays, she learns the truth,
he decides he owes her humility
for the rest of his natural life
and she agrees with him.

Y M B A T S S

A I S I T B O Y E

S F A T M W Y S

I B W L F Y

I G T N T S I Y E

0

You must be able to see something.

All I see is the beauty of your eyes.

Stop fooling around. Tell me what you see.

I'm blind with love for you.

I'll get the needle. There's something in your eye.

Fire

In the morning after the fire
the wind-blown brush around our house
was gray with ash. I could feel
the grit on the carpet and tile but couldn't
see it. The lime-sherbet carpet always pale
anyway, looking beige against the tan walls.
Voluntary evacuations, so we stayed
but kept the windows open for the sound of sirens.
We packed a few things just in case:
Photographs, disks,
no books because how to choose?
I'd die in the fire while making up my mind.

All the journals, too many.
1965 was a good wine, the experience of foreign
travel,
my first big loss. And the notebook in which I kept
special poems, ideas, dreams. The book
my daughter made for me. But how to select other
years,
not to mention all the letters.
Looking at the journals (years to bring them all
together
on the same shelf), I knew there were some
years I wouldn't care to revisit.
Others, I don't know, maybe, or not.
Burn, baby, burn.

And then around midnight
I decided to color my hair. I could see the gray
coming through at the roots. Best to be seen as lime
green

or tan in the overnight shelter, if we had to go.
I couldn't say why it was necessary.
But in the morning when I saw the gray grit and smelled
the ashes on my tongue, I knew
I had wanted to be reborn.
The carpet will never be the same. I can see it fade
in the pale morning sun.
But my own hair is glossy brown, as washed in dew
as my own hair was when the world was new.

Comet

A comet hangs over my head tonight,
dusty with distance and cobwebbed fire.
I ask if it's come for the dinosaurs again.
No, it says--for your daughter.

I would have thought breast cancer
was a small affair, not a colossus of dirty ice
sliding past Jupiter, under the moon,
in locust swarms of biblical proportions.

A poet, I am used to large things writ small:
green that dissolves into gray
and grass that withers
slowly, under the dense weight of air.

I ask questions that I can hold in my hand:
Do apes get breast cancer, and how?
Do hornets get cancer in their stings?
I feel an immense sorrow for cows.

Cancer invades my thoughts: cancer of daisies,
of ferns and mushrooms, eggs and sperm.
All things that divide, all things that die—
kangaroos, cows, and dinosaurs—

and yes, even my one-of-a-kind daughter,
as pure and sinless as the music of the spheres
but just as earthbound, subject to risks and
winnings,
the imperfect chorus of beginnings.

Let her go, I say to the comet, stop your train at my
station.
I'll shovel coal, carry whatever
freight you require: regret, rage, redemption,
witchcraft trials for nonbelievers.

But no, you rush on, stupid train. I wish
I believed in a large hand
that could flick the comet from the sky,
a well-manicured yet lordly hand

that would then go back into its pocket
and let me get back to the conceit of chance.
I can't have a hand only, without the sacred heart,
the horrors of sacred suffering.

No bargain then. No train, no freight.
Nothing I can sacrifice or offer to exchange.
No purpose save to spew out metaphors of pain.
Shut up. Sit under the heavy stars and wait.

Winterspring:
Waiting for the Cancer to Return

This spring did not sing in the same way as
yesterday.
It followed a winter wallow as sprigged and sharp
as decay,
as deep as death is shallow.

The seasons do not reason nor does their
progression follow
a promise to return or mourn. Their wallow signals
change only. If cold now, warm will follow

eventually, or maybe the converse. In a universe
they say all things are constant. How monstrous
to give and give and then unexpectedly reverse.

My words are shallow, my absurdity a curse.
Religionless yet blessed with sin,
I lie with circularity and pray in verse.

Shooting Stars

Stars are eternal
they say. An infernal
way of insuring
eternity. But all
this does is make
children afraid.
When they see
a shooting star, they know,
there is no safety,
none at all,
if even the stars fall.

Elephant Doors

Buying elephant doors is like going
on one of those save-your-marriage athletic jaunts,
like climbing Mt. Everest or swimming across
shark-infested waters. To take a risk
after so many years of settling into a nest,
of predicting reactions and avoiding
all but the most self-evident arguments.
Will he like them? Do I really know?
On the one hand there is the expense
(more than I paid for my first car),
on the other the aesthetics: will he agree
to displace the furniture of our
much-contested use of space? They are
what they symbolize: the elephant in the room.
They rumble in from elsewhere, huge.
The big imagination, the loud trumpet
for renewal and transformation
in the small forest of our end of days.

The Elephant at the Portland
Saturday Market

"Do you like mushrooms too?" I ask the elephant
that appears at the Portland Saturday Market.
The earth sinks under the elephant's feet
and the acorns of the old oaks rattle down
on the keepers of contorted squash and honeycomb,
dried herbs, straw brooms, and mushrooms.
The keepers scream and scatter, leaving a trail
of salt shakers, sandals, scissors, and green combs.
"I prefer mangoes," says the elephant, "hollowed
out
and packed with yogurt. Or so they tell me."
I wonder how the elephant got here, but mostly
why it's so polite. And because it stands there
with the reek of salsa and ginger ale
I take out a Kleenex and brush the acorns from its
head,
the honey from its lips, and only then
does it tell me it prefers bread. "Oh go on," I say.
Such a polite elephant, when offered the mushroom
it tries
to eat it, and then, like Babar's father, dies.

The Auction Shop of the Soul

It is clear that I resist
inheriting a shopping list
of sins and virtues sacrosanct.
I prefer an auction house, a think tank
for negotiating life. To be frank,
I don't think much of virtue or of sin,
but only the taste of breathing:
what is the nature of the air,
whether foul or fair,
an instinct to distinguish courtesy
from authenticity.
And as for love, it is not sex
but loyalty, a magic hex
on the fold of your body that I kiss--
the apex and nadir of our wilderness.

As if There were Anything Else to Do

As if there were anything else to do.
As if meals were important, or garbage,
or making an always unmade bed,
or letting the dog out to the end of his lead.
As if time mattered. As if with your words
you could gather what was scattered,
as if with a twist of an unselfconscious wrist
you could reassemble a shattered mirror.
Such artifice in a saint
approximates absolute zero.
As if heat mattered.
As if there were such a thing as a singular plural.

Archaeological Site

In archaeological sites on abandoned tables
the coffee cups and cereal bowls stand unwashed,
probably by people who would have left anyway
going to the park before the cups are cleaned
then something happened and they never went back.
I look around at the chaos of my living room.
If I never came back it would look
as if disaster had struck and my bones disintegrated
leaving the coffee grounds in the sink
and the pomegranate peels congealing beside
the naked eggs.

This life is whirl and wind,
looking abandoned except that everything's
still up in the air, like a jogger's gear
and only looks abandoned if we disappear.
Home Beautiful is a museum
of reconstructed order. Here
in the long cold shaft of the afternoon
my life divides: the past half done,
the other half that ends too soon--all jumbled,
awaiting order in another eon
through archaeological resurrection.

Lip Balm

We measure out our lives by different means:
by years, by seasons of the moon,
for Eliot by coffee spoons.

I measure mine by lip balm.
Just the other day I bought a box
since in this dry heat, I kept running out.

But as I placed it on the shelf
I thought it seemed a lot.
Will it be here when I am not?

How many years will pass my lips
as inch by inch I pinch it toward my death?
How many cups or gallons smooth my breath?

It's strange to think that these small tubes of gunk
will last beyond my struggling words, my fevered
touch,
will sit there, virgin slime, when I am mulch.

I cannot use it now without a thought
of how much time I have to sip
the wine of days, and touch my finger to my lip.

The Thing That's Missing

I don't remember things
much, and most of them are gone
now. I've got
your basalt letter opener,
the red seed with a hundred
elephants, each for a wish
I've never used. But something
tells me I'm missing something
even though I know
there's nothing worth remembering.
It's all gone, those things
to which I was once linked.
I know because even the things
that are still here could be lost
right now and I wouldn't mind.
It's not as if they were alive.
It's not as if they were kind.

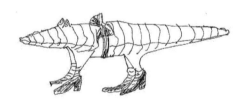

Doing with Less

I'm doing things with less these days.
The house, the food, noblesse oblige,
the way the hips engage and sway,
my heart incapable of siege.

It's not that I don't care. I do.
But language seems more shallow now,
with less of more and more of few,
the chaos of indefinite pronouns.

How it of you or them, they say.
You're breaking up, your language is obtuse.
You toss your words like pebbles in a bay.
Sink or float, what have you got to lose?

I don't mind doing less with more
if what I get is one small candle of desire
to light my solitary way, and yours,
till less sinks down to nothing and expires.

Don't Ask, Don't Tell

In August I disappear
so my birthday can't find me.
It will rub its nose in the scent of my years
and howl on my trail
but I've learned a few tricks.
I shoot out all the lights,
force-feed the cat with cloves,
sneak garlic to the fanged canaries.
I eat all the cherries.
I erase my reflection in the mirror,
pound iron stakes into the dresser,
throw out the French lingerie.
And most of all I block my ears
against the birthday song, against all songs
that remind me that as I grow older, so do you.
You walk closer to the edge than I do.
I hadn't realized how steep the trail is,
how far up we've come.
The ledge narrows as I speak
and I hear the sound of drums.

Sun Break

A sun break they call it, this day of cobalt blue and
sleevelessness,
a dusting of pine pollen on the car's roof,
dragonflies rising
from a swollen stream. Two men with Intel t-shirts
on a wet tennis court.
A luminescent green ball flies over the fence and
lies among
white spring flowers. A team of young men--Asian,
Hispanic, Black—
dribble a basketball too fast to notice who's playing
who.
A man on a bike, baby in a sidecar, daughter on a
new pink bike
and a mother in black spandex holds up the rear.
A man looks like the dog he walks: Great Dane with
expressive eyes
and a combed look. Slugs like discarded condoms
on a wet sheet,
whales among worms. Snails frisk slow-motion on
a hot tin roof.
The air full of white blossoms from the cherry trees,
and you on your knees among the weeds.

OED:
Oxford English Dictionary,
The History (Past and Emergent) of
the English Language

I look for you in the pages of the OED.
It's not words or symbols that I read
but shadows of your smile, the adumbration
of you in my imagination. In between
the spaces of black-blurred words I see
faces and confessions, explosions, de-
compressions. A call to birds;
an epiphany of words.

I use it to avoid stereotypes, the tendency
to think in patterns. You are so unusual
I want to see your shadow,
remind myself of the unusual curve of your cheek.
Remember you as someone unique.
Your interstices, the places in between,
the what you are and what you might have been
if only I could find the right words.
An adjective from whales, a noun from birds.

You cannot be described. No words work.
Then why spend time scavenging discarded
specks of past attempts that leak and lurk
around the edge of consciousness? Because to work
at you is pleasure. As I peel off one more layer,
your carcass shimmers: ghosts of smoke
and wisps of essences are what I measure.

Antithalian:
Opposed to Fun or Festivity
(Half of an Alphabet Song)

Antithalian? Not me. It's just that you
Beguile me with a serious attitude. It's your
Cock-sureness, your embrace of
Death and Buddhist certainty. I love
Each scar, each furrow in your worried face
From which a silent wisdom sings.
Gauntness suits you, my unlikely
Hero. With your zeroes on my tongue,
I feast with kings.

Balter:
To Dance Clumsily

Now I have a word to describe
why I'm altered when we touch.
Rendered brainless by the merest glance.
I stutter-start and shake with lust-slouch
and stammering falter. How can I dance?
I can't even walk. I'll crawl
through the splinters of your smile
over miles of broken stones.
Skinless, I'll dance in my bones.
Skinless, my bones will stutter in the wind
long after you're gone, and on moonless nights
people will hear the sound and say
someone is baltering tonight.

Cellarhood:
The State of Being a Cellar

Of course you're a cellar. I expected
nothing else when I assayed a sashay
down these tripping tippled stairs, but
I hardly expected this state of affairs.
I respect you for your cellarhood.
Believe me, I would
never have expected such floor, such wood,
such lockedness of the door.
Would you let me out? I only came
for a bottle of Faiveley--
a Pinot Noir. You prefer the Merlot?
I find it a bit pretentious. See now,
I've never thought of a cellar
as being quite so self-conscious
of its preferences and personness.
I prefer to take for granted
spaces that are inanimate.
A drink? I like your attitude.
A toast to your cryptic vaultitude,
and to my (hic) sommelierish
vintnerhood.

Chapwoman:
Female dealer or hawker, a trafficking woman

Author of my first chapbook I wondered
if a chapbook were like a chapter in my life,
a stage toward a larger whole (the masterpiece,
the piece of something masterly) but no,
it means only something small
hawked by itinerant dealers or chapmen,
chaps being customers (a contemptuous opinion
implied); to chap, to cheapen, to barter and truck
in a chance way, by the seat of your pants.
And not only that, chapmanable means
fit to be sold. There is no chapwomanable
and if there were, it would probably mean
the special kind of marketing that women do:
that humble undermining of their derring-do,
rooted in body metaphors (what do we traffic in
but sin and sex, small earthly things,
not the Herculean labors of men),
the body vs. the head—now we're back
to chapters, the heads of (corp)orations, capitalists
writing the masterpieces, assigning roles:
an Exaltation of Larks,
a Labor of Moles.

Dracontology:
The Study of Lake Monsters

As if we need more monsters—a plesiosaur
in a teacup of Midwest mud, spotted last Friday
by Old Joe Blow in his Model T, the lake too small
for catfish but what the hey?
Sometimes you gotta believe.

Maybe we're more gullible these days. It's not
like proof is our highest priority. If chance
outweighs reason, why not let tourists flock
to the best sideshow since the Renaissance?
Francis Bacon doesn't need to know

how times have changed. He'd be the first
to revel in the *frisson* of the unknown,
weigh phlogiston, risk being cursed
by priests masquerading as clowns
on the dawn of a new day.

But if he were here, he'd ponder
the size of the monster, the depth of the lake,
how little room there is for wonder. He'd prefer
monsters that require a lot of space.
But you, my heart's desire,

require no ocean voyage, no deep dive.
You are my trial, my knightly test,
the voyage to journey's end. The lies
I tell will hark and hide our happiness.
You are the Snark I dive for.

Epizeuxis:
The Vehement Repetition of a Word

The dawn breaks cold, the color
of disused bronze. The world silent,
an odor of empty closet. Time to leave,
the suitcase packed, the last cup
of coffee drunk, the dregs
left in the sink for someone
who knows how to recycle. I never repeat
my mistakes. One life, one death. Lips shut
to excuses or reversals. I must leave you
here on the windy plateau with
only the howling coyote for company.
I block out his mournful tune,
His yes, his no, and the endless refrain
I love you I love you I love you.

Finifugal:
Shunning the End of Anything

For your last meal from the OED
I serve you *finifugal*. I shun you
as I shun the end of a good book. I neglect
to turn out the light, keep saying,
"Oh this is a good one" as I scan the page
for one more word to keep you here. I laugh longer
and encourage you to talk between bites.
I practice abstinence of time,
mince words and eat each second slowly.
I shun your absence as you measure me for mine.

Goat-Drunk:
Made Lascivious by Alcohol

What an insult to goats who don't need drink
to copulate. They need no adjectives or cocktail
spurs
to stir their lust. They meet, they mate. No need to
think
of promises; no ringed exchanges need occur.
But you and I are sheep, my dear,
so thirsty for each other's words, we hesitate
to drown the sound of language in our cups.
We're bundled up in woolen metaphors. You tup
me with a simile. You make me think.
Naked, ye clothe me with a poem.
I am thirsty and you give me drink.

Heterophemize:
To Say Something Different from What you Mean to Say
Or:
How to break up with someone who doesn't speak your language

"You are like a jellyfish," I said to an old boyfriend.
I meant to say jelly donut, but I knew I misspoke
when he replied that the group word for jellyfish
was bloat.

"You're wrong," I said. "A bloat is a group
of hippopotami. Jellyfish run in smacks."
"I thought it was coyotes that run in packs,"
he said. I said, "A rout." "A what?"
"A rout of coyotes, a wisp of snipe,
a shiver of sharks, a mischief of mice."

He said, "It's hard to talk to you."
"A labor of moles, my love?" "This is absurd.
You never say what you mean."
"I am a dissimulation of birds, perhaps? A siege
of cranes? I would prefer to be
a charm of magpies." But in the end,
in the unmeeting of minds and the lack of havens,
I turned out to be an unkindness of ravens.

Lectory:
A Place for Reading

At last! A word for my favorite place.
Although you consider this a waste of space,
I covet it and refuse to allow
non-reading items to accumulate.

No Kleenex boxes, phones, or food;
no couch with TV set or room for two.
I love the loneliness of lying fallow,
without wings or window view.

Just words, a place set off for reading.
Vampirish, I read like feeding.
Leave me alone when I'm in heat
for books and the sense of a world that's healing.

Open a book and stop the clocks.
Coat the walls with rugs and socks.
Don't wait up and please don't peek
at the page where they finally reveal the plot.

A place where you wash is a lavatory,
for scientific work, a laboratory.
But if your need is for a place to read,
then hector your protector for a lectory.

Noceur:
A Person Who Stays up Late at Night

In the morning I wash clean the dreams, fold them,
put them away for the day. I tiptoe
around the quiet house, fix coffee, write
poems while I listen to you sleep. You snore,
but that's the good news. It's the times you're quiet
that I think about how you've been up all night,
the heaviness of all those regrets
that press down, like the Old Hag, on your chest;
your memories of betrayals, all those lost, few
found.
If I am matitutinal, you are a noun.

Peristeronic:
Suggestive of Pigeons

You hate costume parties, call them moronic--
words are about the only game you play.
I went alone; said I was peristeronic,
which shut people up. I hopped away
from one hawk after another, my left wing
scarred by attacks. I sat in a corner,
choosing hunger rather than sing
for my supper. I thought of you, a loner
with no tendency to fly in flocks,
who with a single glance can stop the clocks.

Some people are pigeon-like: group-loving, gray.
They live in lofts, prefer to eat from hands,
rise shrieking up to greet the dawn of day.
They shit a lot, eat dirt, and go about in bands.
You don't like pigeons but I think that
when you see death, the killing of a child,
you'd like to be a peristeronic rat,
a gray band, all wings and shit-wild.
You are not a pigeon but I'll use one to explain
what you are not: Someone who looks up and
drowns in rain.

Quomodocunquize:
To make money in any way possible
(Thank you, T.S. Eliot)

Let us go then, you and I,
to where the moneylenders quomodocunquize,
like Monopoly players rolling dice across a felt-
lined table.
Let us go and fabricate ill-gotten gains,
the radioactive rains
that follow greed as does the night the day
and saturate our pristine farmlands with decay.

In the room the women come and go
talking of interest rates and quid pro quo.

But wait, my love, what is it?
Let me my memories revisit.
Methinks I think of other guys,
not you, who quomodocunquize.
In fact, you manage the reverse:
In face of want, you open up your purse.

The poker-playing mania you once indulged in
petered out because you never liked to win.
Luck licked your cheeks and gave you wondrous
hands
you never played; you left your money in,
were grateful when you lost, and stood the rounds
so that when all the chips were in
you always left with less than when you came,
less preference for penury than an antipathy to gain.

And indeed there was a time
when Monopoly was played inside the home,
fake money passed around in democratic harmony.
There was a time, there was a time
that our daughter played to win with great intensity.
By owning Boardwalk, railroads, and utilities,
she fought to dominate the market as a single entity.
But when she lost, you said it was a crime,
and offered to extend to her a loan.
A loan for her, a loan for me,
and loans until you gave it all away
and undermined the game as silly play
until we gave it up for toast and tea.

In the room the women come and go
talking of inheritance and status quo.

And indeed there was a time
to wonder, when your mother died,
"Do I dare to leave it all behind?"
To give up all as heir apparent
(they will say, "How this heir is such a fool!")
and subdivide the spoils among the sycophants,
and give away your mother's jewels
so that your brother could be cared for.
He was all you lived for.
And in the end he died
and was buried without fanfare or a stone.
All you have in compensation is this poem.

I know you well, have known you more than half
my life,
as sweetheart, friend, as lover and as wife.
I have measured out your soul with coffee spoons,
have drunk your measure with a heady swoon.
I know your voice as if it were my own.

• • •

So how should I presume?

So how shall I presume to write
of generosity and lack of spite,
of kindness like a perfume on your skin,
of eyes that catch and judge all details even as they
dim?
Of age and living small and giving
flowers for the dead and living,
asking nothing in return?
In Renaissance times you would have burned;
in earlier times been crucified, a saint upon the
sands—
no one trusts a generous man.

And has it all been worthwhile, after all,
now that you see the writing on the wall,
now that the river narrows toward its end
and you watch the ocean for the salmon's run.
And what if after all the gifts, the love, the sacrifice,
no ship appears upon the far horizon
and you die alone?
My death you could bear, but not that of your child.
Oh life, impersonal forces of the wild,
be merciful.

Vergangenheitsbewaltigung:
Coming to Terms with the Past

A single word, like a dust pan, to sweep up
the bits and pieces of the past: some teeth,
cartilage and femur,
a cuplike patella filled with old blood,
half a cranium shattered like an eggshell.
I found them while digging my garden,
trying, like Voltaire, to focus on the present,
on the friends who are still alive, the children
who write from Pittsburgh and come
for visits in the summer. They sit on the old
sofa close to the window and sometimes the sun
hits their blond hair and my eyes glisten
as I remember the Hitlerjugend,
their songs and fierce pride—not because
I thought they were beautiful but because
no one asks. They think
I am crying over spilt milk, but in fact
I cry because there is milk now, and beets
in the garden, and uncensored letters,
no need to watch others for their lies,
and when I lift my arm in the air it is only
to keep the sun from my eyes.

Visuriency:
The Desire of Seeing

Every rose, each sunset, every star
in its blue-black background. Street lights
in fog, a pregnant cat in a rubbish yard,
a black streak of sparrow, a bulge
of robin, a jet's trail lacy in a cold sky.
Your uncovered ears, reddish brown;
a gray stubble of beard. That mole
on the top of your shiny head. Bed
at dawn, blue gray. The way you walk
naked in the dark.

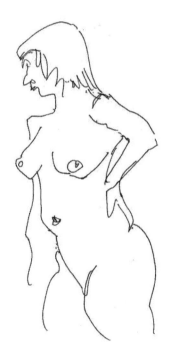

Well-Lost:
Lost in a Good Cause

I have a good sense of direction. On a scale
of one to ten I do better than a GPS
in finding my way through neighborhoods,
and don't need an atlas in the murky woods
of Dante. My inner compass knows
up from down and east from west.
I am rarely surprised by lost horizons,
which is too bad. I like the feeling
of lostness, the stagger, the reeling
of sense out of time and space,
the feeling I get when I look at your face.
For you I'd lose myself, turn topsy-turvy,
the way I get lost in a book, a chapter, a single
word.

Xerostomia:
A Dryness of the Mouth Caused by Insufficient Production of Saliva

Comparing her father to salt was not such a good
idea
for Cordelia. If you were my father
I would have compared you to water.
Mother, father, friend, lover—
90% of us is water
which we usually ignore except
when it's in excess (like sweat
and vomit and tears). So prolific
is the body that we seldom explore
words that describe its lack.
Do not say, my king, that I adore
you for your salty flavor (which I do)
but that you are the ocean in which I am intact.
I am a desert without you.

Zeroable:
May be Omitted from a Sentence
Without Loss of Meaning
(The Other Half of an Alphabet Song)

Just because you spout zeroes on your
Knuckering tongue, my anti-social lover,
Let it not be said that you are a
Monster best left to languish under water.
No matter how many meals I've scorched
Or poems left unfinished because of your
Pride, your undiminished capacity for
Quarreling to make a point, I would
Rather side with you and put the world's
Schnoz out of joint because without you
Terabytes are miniscule, infinity
Untenable. Face it, my favorite Buddhist,
Value isn't nothing. In the rainforest of
Words, your disciplined negativity is
Xerotic. For all your foibles,
You are not
Zeroable.

Discovering a Beautiful New Word

When Columbus discovered the egg
of a new world, he carved magic runes
on its shell and ignored the name
it called itself. He drew maps,
the blank spaces filled with seas of pearls
and clouds of golden rain, the wrong
kind of Indians riding elephants. He grew fat
and died of indigestion. Anyone knows
when you eat words without meaning,
they are like plastic bubble wrap, a row
of vacuum snacks you can't stop popping though
they lie in your stomach like heavy zeroes.

I Get Lost Slowly

I get lost slowly, arriving at the place
I've defined as lost, but it's no use.
My mind's a map. Fictional, I know,
but close enough. I'm not really trying
to get lost, just avoid the trap
of knowing where I want to go.

Where to Stay for the Night

Where to stay for the night
is one of those ways to assess
personality. Are you a Ramada Inn
or a Marriott Suites, two beds or one,
the hard kind with the magic fingers or the one
that sinks to frame your body?
Mini bar or coffee? ships on the wall or fruit?
The top floor with a long view
or something close to the exit,
no elevator required? I like huge rooms
with a lot of space. The best
was one in the dead of winter, an old
beer-making factory near the Lake District.
The floor was uneven, as I found out
in the night. Like negotiating a bumpy sea.
But the best was a small room in Rome:
white walls, narrow bed, a black crucifix
with shadows on white plaster.
A nunnery in a red light district.
Cloistered silence in a dark night.

Catalonian Asphodel

Fools all! who never learned
how much better than the whole the half is,
nor how much good there is
in living on mallow and asphodel.
--Hesiod

Frugality and mystery:
off the cinnamon-colored street,
behind thick walls a garden.
The leather-palmed widow sears
luncheon on a tripod:
mullet, fig and asphodel.
A trickle of dark wine,
a table of maiolica tiles
brushed with lemon-scented sprigs of rosemary.

The oboe of old Catalonian tunes
blows eerie off the dustblown fields while I
lie under a fleur-de-lis quilt
and a scarlet damask sky:
a tourist anarchist who hums of goat-kings
trysting with fellowship and austerity.

Paper-thin scales of memory
like those on mackerel and anchovy
float through dreams like olive oil
beneath the fleur-de-lis--
the elusive scent of cinnamon
and thyme on an onion-tinted sea.
Here in the gingery Catalonian night
it feels right to speak of mysteries.

But kings, surfeited, sink on seas, and no true anarchists
sleep under the fleur-de-lis.
They sleep beneath an animistic tree
on plants they praise and eat,
and when they emigrate
search through the thymeless city streets
for watercress and dill,
for fish with bones and birds that fly
against the window drunk on juniper. Yet still

(not king nor anarchist, no neolithic
keeper of the asphodel but merely poet)
I listen for oboes
and look for larks and uncut amethyst,
aurora borealis in the mist,
the disembodied charm of Catalonia
in rue and myrtle shrub and tamarisk

while eating meat and drinking store-bought wine
and sleeping under sheets. In Catalan
the voice of the turtle is heard across the land,
and death is sea salt and a knife to carve
up dreams. But in my lemon-scented bath I hear
the voice of Celeano crying:
you will never find the city of your dreams
until you starve.

Frauenkirche, Dresden, 1945

Stained glass: an aftermath
of cut skin and sin.
Remember the glorious holies
with the sun shining through their skin,
their shining follies
illuminated from within
and their brittle bodies
lead-sheathed against the wind.

Remember, for the fire boiled
the martyrs in their savage arc.
But these masters of *trompe l'oeil*,
war masters of the purple heart
and burning vermillion
melted long before the start
of bent foil and cut skin.
They made death an art.

Thin glass like human flesh: made on a bed
of clay and mercury.
The virgin skin, encased in lead,
baked to translucent mystery
lends structure to the dead.
Wanton and remote, this beauty
hangs like a word unsaid,
breathless in the metallic corset of the sky.

I wonder what song the martyrs sang
when the bombs awoke
their base beauty. Where cut glass hangs
the sun weeps. The earth spoke
of reformation, the language
of hope, a voice so high, brittle, and cold
it pierced the heavens. As the angels ran
for cover, their wings broke.

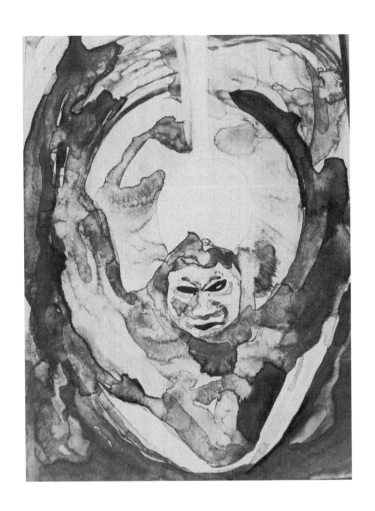

Chatwin's Songline

The moment I died I came back here
to the land of the dilly-bag, the eucalyptus inhaler,
with a matt-black abo singing of waterholes.
This wasn't the place I expected to go.

Patagonia would have been my preference,
or Kashmir where I fell in love and broke my vows.
I was an iron man in search of rust,
with an appetite for loneliness. But now

I'm stuck on a lizard hill with a Walbiri elder
whispering in my ear
that my Death Dreaming needs to be sung.
Just walk, he said, you'll know it when it comes.

Those songlines the abos are always going on
about—
the land is the song and all that rot—
how they sing the world into being.
I'm English and do better with a compass and a map

which I don't have, of course, being dead. All I
have
is my lust for wandering. The abos would have said
my mother was aboard a ship when I first kicked,
and a sea-going Ancestor gave me the taste

for salty stories and a nomadic song. That's why
I've never settled any place. Or maybe it's the
English desire

to encompass the world, to leave our footprints everywhere--
our way of singing ownership with fire instead of voice.

I'm in a dry place now. The cattle lie
with their legs in the air, black with hungry crows.
This is no place for cattle, only honey-ants and abos.
This is Muralinga where the British set off the H-bomb

and opened up the deep caves where the maggot flies
were imprisoned by a long-ago Ancestor. All who walked
through the cloud lost their tongues. The land itself dies
when its songs are no longer sung.

We must hate ourselves to leave ourselves behind,
always on the lookout for a better origin.
Isn't that what home is?—a place that's worthy of returning to,
a place where the bones make way for you.

Oh father who birthed me, and the fathers who came before,
shed a little light on the dark space where I've made my bed.
There are stories here in the history of my bones.
I'm an Iliad on a Walkabout in search of home.

Summer Solstice, Achill Island, Ireland

Soft sets the sun in Achill.
The carrigeen moss in the silver bay.
The bell-hung stems of the foxglove.
The sheep leap high in the new-mown hay.
The oil's in the peat by the spade-cut rows.
The mica, the moss, and the shrieking crows.
When the dark sets down like a leaking sieve
you can see the bonfires of Achill.

The flames flare up and the ashes fly
in billowing smoke to the spreadeagle sky--
old tires and timber, broken rakes,
the children dance on a makeshift stage.
Pass the sausage around with the cake and the
cream.
The high-stepping dancers in emerald green.
The smallest, the gladdest, the saddest colleen
is touching the stars in Achill.

The crab claws scuttle in Achill.
The bones of the eagle lie deep.
Drowned voices pray in Bleanaskill Bay.
The host of Cuchulain's asleep.
Though the nettles grow taller than falling stones
and the Famine's a voice in the storm,
the sky is still light in the heart of the night
and bright burn the bonfires of Achill.

Black Water

Sailing to Anacapa over green waves,
the glint of gold in shallow coves,
we passed the continental shelf into black water
where molten lead cast glints of quivering silver.
This is not the glitter of quick gold, no,
but the far star hard fire stuff of the deep old--
here where the earth drops off
and the water changes color from green to black—
no more sand, no forests of kelp, just deepness
steeped in coldwater waves that do not break--
headed for Anacapa, an island without water,
where coreopsis and singing lizards and island
foxes
drink marine dew and stew in their strangeness.
I spend all my time there listening for you
in your farness, my friend who has gone on without
me
on the low road under the sea. Out here, without
surf,
I sink down deep and walk with the kraken,
drink his blood and eat his pearls.

Castaway

Not rooted nor cast from native land
I set my net for trout or eel,
the pole generic, the cast between
what I almost see and almost feel.

Lonely for Coleridge's frost,
specific constellations overhead,
I lust for what limits I've lost,
what makes an unmade bed.

I cast for the big fish that lives
nowhere, cast as I must
as a blind man would. I care
for the interstices of dust.

Nowhere is not anywhere. I do not
wander for its own sake
but quest for things unsaid. This knot,
conundrum of the commonplace

is stubborn, unromantic. Where
I fall and flail is somewhere in between
the trout and eel, the flounder's stare,
the watery land in which I cannot breathe.

I cast off parents. Let me be
word-scuttled, witless, and unmade,
not fish nor foul decree
of body, neither particle nor wave,

that cat of Schrodinger with Cheshire grin—
what would I choose if I were him?
I'd steal his smile and let his body fade
to light, to the light cast, away.

Oregon

In the beginning: a rumor, a northwest mist,
land of cedar tangle and fern-firs, fish.
A place where the barns have signs like Organic
Food
and Hand-spun Yarn and Daffodils. A place of
seeds
with a research center for turf. The sky pools with
rain
like the world's going to end, and suddenly
there's all that cerulean, and you drive through
rainbows. Blue houses on yellow hills.
Signs by the clear-cut say Real Wood Furniture.

A place where you see someone you know on the
train
going in the opposite direction, reading a book,
and children are encouraged to wave at strangers.
The Voodoo Donut shop offers coffin-shaped
pastries
in pink boxes. A restaurant calls itself Veritable
Quandary
in lieu of a name the owners could agree on.
At the local Denny's they offer a bacon
maple sundae—like many things in Oregon,
better in the conception than the execution.

A place where the Sylvia Beach Hotel is not named
after a beach
but the woman in Paris who published James Joyce
and kissed Hemingway at the end of the war.
Where each
room has a theme, like Ogden Nash and Tolkien, or

the Poe Room with its ravens and pendulum above
the bed.
The sign on the Gertrude Stein Room that says
"When I arose a rose." And the woman at the front
desk
teaches you a cat's cradle her father taught her,
and cries when the next year you remember.

Where people know the names of the five hundred
species
of birds that nest around Portland, like the Swifts
that take off from chimneys in the spring
and people picnic on the grass to watch.
Where a cheese factory is as popular as Disneyland.
Where a tiny town in the Cascades
puts on a Morris Dance for Mother's Day
and a poet at the end of the Northwest Poets
Concord says
I feel I've had all the bacon I can eat.

Evolutionary Haiku

Love is not for snakes.
For mammals, warmth is solar
endo-thermostat.

Love is not for birds.
Some mammals risk with sonar:
No-net acro-bat.

Love is not much fun.
Short-term exploding nectar:
High-heat ecto-splat.

Asian Carp

Who
would
have thought
that fish would leave
their element with such force,
as if trying to fly, or perhaps
they have always
harbored a wish,
a yen (so to speak)
to slap
fishermen

Spider

Spider hangs his web
from the tip of the new moon
casting thin shadows

The Thing with Feathers

Plumes, feathers, whole birds on hats,
suddenly every woman in the city wanted
what Emily Dickinson expressed. Not just
the feathers of peacocks and parrots and parakeets
but the Good Lord Bird itself,
its three-foot wingspan beating wind from hell
and its ivory beak ripping off bark
and making the pines bleed. One was captured,
brought back to a hotel room where it demolished
a table, two chairs, and a wall
before it died. But the artist drew it,
and packed it with cotton, and it lives
forever in the Smithsonian, a stiff reminder
of the dangerous, the beautiful, and the extinct.
They say it lives on in Alaska
which was never part of its habitat
but hope springs eternal in unlikely places.

Falling Bodies

The greatness of Galileo was not that he stood alone
like a fixed beacon of truth among the heavens
but that he fell (a shifty, oleaginous stone)
into the murky waters of central motion,
      rebutting the static perfection
        of Aristotle and the Inquisition.

The Greeks, like the Inquisition, played up statics:
keeping things steady. Stones fell in search of
ground
and flames leaped skyward, attracted
to the empyrean of their original home.
      Every object had its perfect place.
      Motion was an absurd state.

God's blueprint for the world required
no motion. Simultaneously thought and birthed
were frogs and unicorns and lice,
all shaped from air and water, fire and earth.
      With God stable in his firmament,
      why bother with the messy business of
measurement?

Aristotle did one thing right:
he set himself up for a fall,
the power of his logic so precise
that he prepared the world to prove him wrong.
      Aristotle spun theories that could be tested.
      Only the outcome was unexpected.

His hypothesis that falling bodies flow
At a speed proportionate to their weight

is easy to test: drop the gluttonous Galileo
with the scrawny Aristotle off a cliff. The debate
        will be settled by their simultaneous descent
        (with little time to crow or to repent).

And if Aristotle is wrong about falling bodies,
perhaps he's wrong about the Great Chain of Being,
that all things have their perfect place. Perhaps God
himself
does not exist. Perhaps the Inquisition
        like Aristotle cannot resist motion.
        To fall or not is not the question,

because falling is all there is: a great dance
of danger, relativity, and chance.
But the crafty Galileo knew
that he could have his cake and eat it too:
        that under the apparent chaos of the long
fall,
        motion is fixed in formula and law.

The greatness of Galileo was not that he stood
alone,
committed to the truth of central motion
(threatened by torture, he denied all),
but that, while he spent his life like a fixed star,
        his ideas fell through ecumenical minds,
        gaining speed and distance over time.

Quaternion

A quaternion was locked in a room.
'Twas simple of them to assume
      that if three were complex,
      the fourth was a real set
of additive cogito sum.

Worn To Perfection

A bird's beak stays the right length
through use, unlike a pen
worn down to the nib; unlike a body
worn out by too much exercise.
Unlike the bird's beak, pen, or body
is the heart,
which enlarges to enclose the world
and can only be
broken.

Lonely Hearts Ad
for the Humanly Challenged

Lonely widow seeks S&M relationship with male.
Communicate by web only.

Paston's Romance

In Paston's 15th-century England, love was given
second place to land and wealth and power.
To marry up or down, the contracts sought
to bind alliances by debt or dower.

The old, decrepit, and unfit
were wed to children, maidens sacrificed
to family pride. No bonds were sacred
if unsuitable or highly priced.

With few exceptions--but there were a few
for whom all calls of duty rang unheard
in ears gone dumb, struck silent by a sun
that savaged custom and made caste absurd.

Across all boundaries, defying rules,
love blossomed, sere and strange among the flocks--
as stark, as incandescent as the moon
consuming sanity and stealing time from clocks.

A month, a year and more the lovers waited,
kept by outraged families in the dark,
with beatings, threats, and outrage all compressed
in letters to the future. Bitter, stark,

and drear these days must once have been
to her who waited, wept, and doubted
that her love would yet to her be true
when all was said and done. If caste is flouted,

who can tell by what strange compass
steers the heart? These were days
when Brendan voyaged to a far Brazil,
and islands shifted in the haze,

where dragons sang and seaweed tides converged
on sinking ships, around which danced blue light
of gryphons, goddesses, and cannibals--
where only the Pole Star of the heart could pierce
the night.

So by this thin magnetic line they stayed
plumb and true, though out of whack with gravity
that bore them down--until disgorged between
the Pillars of Middle Ocean, into the Darkness Sea.

Dogwood

Black bark winter, skeleton dog.
Bark, dog, bark in the cold
while spring creeps up your skinny limbs
and forces green into your fingertips.
Little yellow toenails dig through digits,
grow white palms that glisten in rain,
ears cocked to the wet wood. Food
for club-gall midges and seed-corn maggots
and scale with its cotton wisps dropping tar
on your flowers and fruit, the larvae
sharing your veins as you hum
to the summer coming, as you
spin white platters in the dusk
and burn like a candle down to its yellow nub,
all the wax melted down on a plate,
a pat of white warm butter on a limp green leaf.
Understudy to the forest pack of hardwood trees,
you are hard enough.

Police Report

The police report says a man
broke into a house in Fresno
where two farmers lived. He rubbed one down
with spices and whacked the other with a sausage
before fleeing. The police report doesn't say
what spices the farmers had or what they used them
for.
So many questions and suggestions (the sausage
is compelling, Freud would say). I wouldn't mind
being rubbed with sage (but not cinnamon), to smell
of the desert
after rain. And as for the sausage
I'm okay with that, as long as it's sheathed in
casings. But back
to the farmers, let's assume there were words
exchanged, reference to mothers and sires,
the insult of whom requires seasoned words and
fire.

In the Shadow of the Red Wheelbarrow

Much depends on the red wheelbarrow, they say,
but what about the used condom after the roll in the
hay?—
which has as much to do with free love
as the red wheelbarrow has to do with a philosophy
degree.
Both have to do, indirectly,
with relationships: the no or the yes yes yes,
to life without threat of exhausted death
after fourteen children like our grandmothers did.
In the shadow of the red wheelbarrow, superego or
id?
Both are true. In the red bed let me lose my head
without being a furrow for the red wheelbarrow.
Did not the carpenter cut wood, bend nails,
choose only one of many colors? In the odors
of a woodshop, sanctity smells like shit.
Get out of my life and let me get on with it.

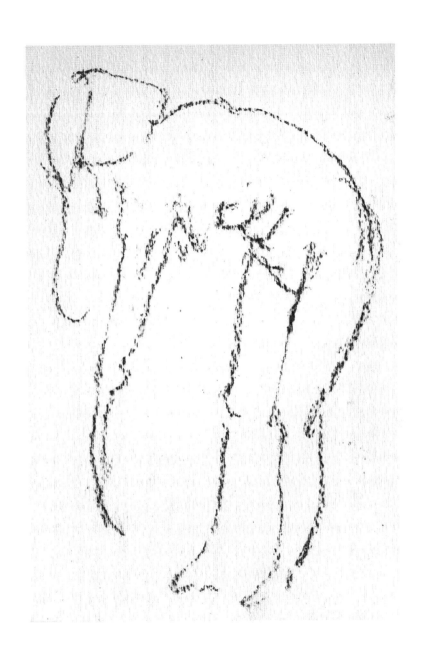

Valley Girl Villanelle

It's like, you know, I never
cared to get a degree. My parents had their Ph.D.'s
but I, like, didn't care. Whatever.

It's like you know you have to go to school forever
but who cares? My parents got their Ph.D.'s
and didn't care, like, whether

I stayed in school or liked it, never
asking. To what degree should a kid care
if they live or die or get a Ph.D.? Whatever

they said I didn't hear and didn't care.
To what degree I cared they never
like, you know, cared. Whatever.

After the Sunspots

After the sunspots my toenails turn yellow
and a tongue grows from my shoulder
as if the cosmic explosions have scrambled the order
of parts. A third eye creeps down my nose
and gets caught between my teeth
where it reports on the carbohydrate index,
informs on the ratio of broccoli to butter.
I wish I had an eye on the bottom of my foot
so I could see the landscape close up.
Speak of perspective! Here's mud in your eye.

Sestina for an Alien's Feet

A man came to our village on naked feet.
How could he walk so far, we wondered,
we who walk on craggy shores,
climb cliffs with iron-clad toes wrapped in leather.
We could tell he came from a far land
and would have killed him for his open soles

except for the women who liked the idea of
revealing soles
to strangers who have never seen each other's feet,
who have never stepped off their father's land
nor stopped to wonder
if there are alternatives to iron and leather,
and whether, somewhere, there are silken shores

that caress our lonely limbs and shore
up the spirit against those toe-stubbing souls
that would sacrifice grace for leather.
Some shed their shoes, as if by embracing defeat
they could develop the capacity for wonder
and consider the possibility of another land

from which iron is banned. To land
always on the spiny ribs of craggy shores
defines our manhood. If you wonder
or wander too much, your soles
may be burned with fire, and your feet
cut off. But the women argued that the leather

of souls is of sterner stuff, if leather
is the measure of what we treasure. Oh land
quietly if you care about the alien's feet,
they cried. Look how he leaves his blood on the
black shore,
the same rust-hue as ours. It's the soles
of his feet that make me wonder

what he is: animal, vegetable, mineral. I wonder
if he can speak through the three mouths in his
leather
chest or if they are the repository of souls,
like the holes we dig in the land
so that children washed out beyond our shores
can find their way home on their leather-clad feet.

He fills me with wonder, this stranger from
a strange land
without leather, so vulnerable as he lies on
our shores
and sings through the soles of his naked feet.

The Thames is Just a River

The Thames is just a river:
water, muck, the debris
of lives. Pocahontas and Tiberius,
Shakespeare inventing Hamlet and Lear.
Garbage. Raleigh's new pipeweed.
Crockery, bones, hawk-spit.
Pollen on the gray water.
Misty boats lined up to the horizon
beyond which lie the Hesperides
whose garden glows with orbs of magic oranges.

The Thames is just a river
with a source from nothingness, a spring or two,
a wave with a tide and underbelly
that coughs up broken crockery,
not wide enough to lose the other side,
not clear enough to see the bottom,
flowing with disappointments and beginnings,
baptisms of drunken revels, aftermaths
of storms. Wash off the toffee stains and blood.
Don't lean too far or dance on the wobbly bridge.

Pocahontas on the last leg of her journey
back to Virginia, her small son
cradled on her hot breast, might have said
Oh river whose waves are deep and brown,
carry me out to sea and home. Or maybe
she just died and the river flowed on,
with its low tides and high, its journeys and
endings,
its lost rings and thrown hats, and on rare mornings,
miracles. The Thames is just a river.
A poem is just a poem.

Cinquain

Poem:
Wordsliver mayhem,
Remembering, ululating, stimming,
Dishwater gold explodes sideways.
Wordplay.

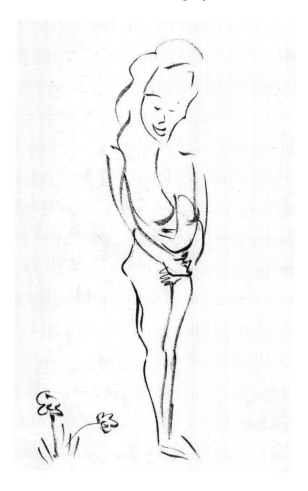

Tag and Release

Books strategically abandoned in public places.
If you find such a book
on a bus or train or beach
do not look around guiltily for an absentminded
reader.
You may take it with impunity,
like finding a puppy in a cardboard box
barking its head off till you pick it up
and tuck it under your coat where it grows
warm and silent, waiting to be loved.
It's cold in the unreading world
of illiterate snakebite salesmen and entrepreneurs
who would sell you something without the fine
print.
The books, once sent to landfills or third world
countries
are now being released into our own headwaters,
to filter the murky assumptions about evolution,
death panels, and birthers. So private,
these pages of public domain,
this rare beast almost extinct,
a literary freak released upon the trickling tide.
May you live. May you find a home.
May you grow, migrate, and return tenfold.

A Poem Should Make You Itch

A poem should make you itch
where you hadn't thought to scratch;
it should tag things you'd forgotten there were
words for.
It should nab infatuations,
help you name the constellations,
build the stations of the cross that others bleed for.

A poem should lacerate,
flense the whales and wake the kraken
where it sleeps in fathoms deep and uncontested
until wakened by incessant
repetition of inflections
and dissolves in verbal bioluminescence.

Out of puns and rhymes demotic
we'll construct a rule despotic:
that you must devour at least a poem a day.
This should separate the heroes
from the zombies and the zeroes
as they feed upon the detritus of fate.

A poem isn't food.
It's the rhythm in your blood.
It's the tintinnabulation of remorse.
     It's the universal tidal table—
     catch the waves if you are able—
     drown inside the human fable--
If you cannot ride a memory
or round up singularities
with words, perhaps you'd better ride a horse.

A poem should make you scream
in the places where you mean,
where you mean not what you said but what you
meant.
          It will never satisfy you, please
          the hounds of war, get rid of fleas, or
          dim the tide of concupiscence,
          dull the ache, the itch, the essence
of the accident that's always present
from our birth to our senescence—
poetry, our bane, our king of chaos, pope of dreams.

Emily Dickinson's Dog

Emily Dickinson sits alone
condensing her woes, abstracting gloom--
her counterpoint rhythms a bone
to the dog that lives in her room.

The world outside has its own affairs--
heroic, chatty heights of lore.
But the dog is dumb and keeps its lair
in the cave of her soul.

She keeps no company but his
and waits with bitter wine
for him who could but will not come
in this or any other time.

A soul of grace will close the gate
and throw away the key--
with metaphor, the game of words
for company.

The dog needs constant exercise
and Emily's hand is sore.
He runs for miles in fettered skies
but never passes the door.

Chasing Rabbits
"He who chases two rabbits catches none"
(Chinese fortune cookie)

You like to chase rabbits—admit it—
a flash fiction here, a play and poem there,
a short story written between book chapters.
All urgent, clamoring to be done,
all crying, Pay attention!
The problem with rabbits is that they run
in different directions.
You have to change tactics,
a slow roll or a flying tackle,
a bow and arrow, handcuffs, a knife
that cuts three ways; slow food
vs. barbecue.

Besides, the taste
doesn't live up to the chase,
not to mention having to clean them if they're
caught.
By the time you get around to the final eating,
they taste like sweat. They've been spiced and
beaten,
dredged in butter and super-fried.
That's why you spend so much time
reading cookbooks. You know
the rabbits will get away, your hands
will be empty, your taste buds yearning
for the difference between the imagined taste
and the real thing.

When Asked What I Write

A tale, as in the accumulation of events,
first one thing happens, then another.
An accounting, as if there is some
explanation for all this, not random
happenings, and also a moral
to the story. Not just life going on
and on but toward a goal, hence tale,
as in tally; counting our life like coffee spoons,
marching toward doom, which is better
than random evolution. But that's not
what I'm doing. Maybe I'm writing
a saga, as in sage, an old woman's view
of family lives and battles—but no, I couldn't care
less (what an odd phrase, does it mean
I could care more?). A bird's eye view
of lives seen from a distance and told in rhyme.
But really, I'm just pushing words around
in my room: a noun here, a verb there, like growing
mushrooms.

It Takes as Long as it Takes

Believe what you like about old age,
it's unpredictable and slow.
It takes as long as it takes.

In a stumbling rush, when young, to create
a legacy (of what I did not know),
I believed what I liked about old age:

that living long compounded failure and mistakes;
that the old should leave when it was time to go.
It takes as long as it takes

for the young to modify mistakes, so hungry are
they
for success. Their children watch them come and
go,
and forge their own beliefs about old age.

My children taught me how to tolerate
their own and my impatience. Now I know
it takes as long as it takes.

I sit here with my words upon the page,
a lifetime spent with words both pale and slow.
Believe what you like about old age,
a poem takes as long as it takes.

Canzone for Leonard Cohen

If I could sing to you, I'd sing
of leaves of gold, their burnished blades
too bright to see. The mesophyll
of heaven's in your veins,

an aphrodisiac of words. If I
could sculpt your likeness, it would be
of fire and air, of earth and ice
and scarred with tears, as ugly

as a worm inside a heart. I'd drape
a molten shroud of silk against the setting sun
and watch it burn. You give, you take,
you saturate my soul with what you've sung

and leave me drowning in your human hymn.
Forget the midrib flow of molten gold,
the blade, the margin, and the petiole.
Forsake all other leaves. Praise him.

Where Will my Poems Go?

Where will my poems go when I'm dead?
Not the chapbooks, the hand scribbled notes
but the ones I haven't written yet.
Where will the half-lit words go? Will they burn
when my flesh is cremated or escape
through the crevices of the eyes and add to the
ozone?
Will they live on like a layer of unlived skin,
these poems I've imagined but never lived in.
Perhaps I should be buried under my books, like
stones
to hold me down until the poems I've never written
rise up from the earth and kindle my bones.

Scissors

She starts a project assembling the necessary tools:
The graph paper and pencils, the rasoplast eraser,
colored paper and ruler. The scissors.
Especially the scissors.
She builds up and cuts back, going small
but deep. Accumulating, refining
the massive outlay, then the final cuts
where almost nothing is left.

Art

Art is accident, angle, an inward
explosion like a light bulb, a forward
impulse, a meeting
of your own mind, suddenly,
as if you'd met a stranger,
a body naked seen from behind—
a fresh view, a new knowing,
an idea on its way to becoming
itself, only more intensely,
more fraught with the inwardly.

Art is the making of a riddle from a solution,
like a ball turned constantly in the hand
as if each turn brought to view a new land, a key
to the cabinet of curiosity
in which reside the bits and pieces of the self--
those jeweled splinters encased in the pitch of a
chaotic sea,
all shimmer and float. Art coats
a bird with incandescent plumage,
digs gold in the cloister with koi, and even
in the shadowy soil of dishwater shows us Eden.

Listen!

Listen! I do not come to bring you arms
against the monster menacing your farms.
I carry no knives and when the dark comes down
I specialize in not being found.

So do not look to me for sword and shield
to fight the horror harrowing your fields
except—be not so hasty to throw me out—
I offer a small skill, the music in my throat.

You ask, quite reasonably, what good is a song?
And you're right, it does nothing at all
to halt the creature creeping through the midnight
corn,
to blunt the sharpness of its thrusting horn

or seal torn arteries and broken bones—
yes, yes, I know the children are listening,
and that's the point and purpose of my singing.
Listen! I'll conjure a sun that burns forever

over an apple grove, a little house, pure water,
a sweet-natured wife and kind-hearted father,
a clever son and beautiful daughter,
who live out their happy days forever after.

Of course brightness itself has its cost. Without
shadows
we forget the dead and what we've lost.

Have faith in the wisdom of children: they only pretend
that the sun never dies and there is no end.
It is not with arms but stories that we fight
the weary parade of days, the endless night.

World Book Night, April 23, 2012

Across the US on this single night,
twenty-five thousand volunteers fan out,
accosting strangers with free books,
assaulting the personal space of commuters
on the 5:30 MAX train, cutting through
their self-absorption at the end of a long day
like a chapter coming to a close.
Happy birthday, Shakespeare,
Happy deathday Cervantes,
birth and death like the first and last lines
of a book, not necessarily a bestseller
but usually long, packed with visual images,
double entendres, and a few puns.
"Happy World Book Night," I say,
"Would you like a free book?"
Suspicion, eye avoidance—no, I'm not
panhandling, not offering religious tracts,
only a slice of the past, Patti Smith's
autobiography, *Just Kids*, of the dawn of punk rock,
of Dylan and Gregory Caruso and Andy Warhol,
the days when Martin Luther King rose and fell,
Robert Kennedy was shot, Charlie Manson
murdered.
Love children of the Haight spread flowers and
AIDS,
and LSD slowed life down to a pulsing crystal
point.
Maybe I am dispensing religious tracts
to the Muslim girl with her head scarf;
to the young woman reading one of those paperback
books

you don't remember five minutes after you finish;
to the couple who speak only Spanish;
to the man with the small daughter who says
"No thanks, I don't have time to read";
to the slim young man on the bicycle who says,
"I travel light and books are too heavy."
To them I say take this book, it costs you
nothing but time. It is a seed that will grow
in your soul; a Pied Piper song
that will lead you on a journey,
one of those songs of nightingale and morning lark,
whose refrain will linger at the end, will resonate,
long after you close the last page, into the dark.

In Praise of Clichés

There is comfort to be had in clichés,
all those tree tops masking the death of a falling
child.
Oh rockabye baby, an apple never falls
far from the tree. Don't ask.
Remember how curiosity killed the cat
and mutton was dressed as lamb being led
you know where. How sweet they are,
these little bludgeons that take to reality
like clods of earth filling an open, hungry mouth.

If We Owned Stories

What would happen if we owned stories
and valued them more than stocks or bonds
or futures in pork snouts. If we valued not how
much a man had when he died
but how well he spoke. If we treasured words—
this one an opal, a diamond, a pearl—
If we thanked each other for new words and
believed
that by giving them away we increased the store
of human wealth. If we hoped for inflation, an
infinite
expansion of treasures added to the great
warehouse of verbal possibility. And each day
we would walk through this warehouse
as if through a waterfall, not a trickle
of guttural stutters for candyfloss, taffy drawn
out and folded with tongues greased
with butter and sugar not bitter
like weeds or the tendons of salted cadavers.
Let us dress our naked hunger with the silks
of metaphors, let down our symbolic hair.
Withdraw the needles from the eyes, sew back the
tongues
on the lambs. Rip off the cataracts,
offer splints, share shoes as we limp ahead
toward the event horizon. Invest in beginnings
that like the snake have already swallowed their
ends.

Blue Horse

In the morning before breakfast, against the dawn's
dazzle,
I saw a woman on a blue horse ride across the
horizon.
She wore a black veil that followed her like smoke,
a gossamer spider's web that caught
the night just gone, the early morning sun.
She might not have existed, might have been
wind among clouds, birds changing direction,
except for the blue horse
that could have been nothing else.

> When there is nothing left to feel,
> When the real is less real than the unreal,
> When time is a clockwork shadow,
> When what I knew I no longer know,
> Then I will keep my eye on the improbable,
> Which as Sherlock Holmes knew was the
> only
> Choice when faced with the impossible.

At the dawn of my twilight I look for myself
draped in gossamer, riding a blue horse.
The world is smoke and wind among clouds,
no more than a flock of birds changing direction.
All I know is that I ride a blue horse
and must go where it goes,
my only certainty a fiction
painted in a color I believe in.

Digging for Daylight

I don't hope for daylight, no,
that would be too much to hope for,
those little pellets of dawn-dragons
drawn across blistered palms,
my shovel-shriven elbow grease of a life,
my digging toward daylight.

No, give me the gray, the midnight black,
the filibustered argument, the last laugh
on the dim side of dawn. I don't want to see
what wounds are cradled in his brief grief,
the aftermath of the deep-dug fight
that shrivels in the face of light.

Little Slant Stories

Tell the truth, said Emily, but tell it slant.
On Photoshop I smudge your pixelled brow
and liquefy your lips. I can't
eliminate what nature won't allow

but I can nudge the truth toward beauty.
When my CPU breaks down
and all I have is short-term memory,
I'll scratch my stories in the ground,

on cave walls and the river's slippery skin.
My message isn't creed, perfection, or their ilk
(no devils, gods, remorse, or sin)
just music: words of wool and silk

that shield your body from the storm
and circulate the blood around the wound.
With pen and paper I will keep you warm.
I'll write down what I know: the lost, the found,

the salamander winding of a river's course,
the little songs that stick like burrs inside the head
and can't be driven out—the secrets of remorse
that uncork wisdom and revive the dead.

      Like matins, like a midnight chant,
      I tell my little stories slant.

Quantum Physics

In 1890 a man shot an Indian
who stood beside the Pacific with his hand
raised in the air, as if to say
hello, goodbye, I am here. A hundred years
later the Indian still stands
by the shore in the photograph
shot by the man. He is here,
he is there, just as he was
on that day. The man who shot him
has vanished, although presumably
he is just as here and there as the Indian,
but we have no evidence
except the assumption of his ghostly finger
on a button that was once a button
and is now a pile of rust, or perhaps
flowers in another universe.

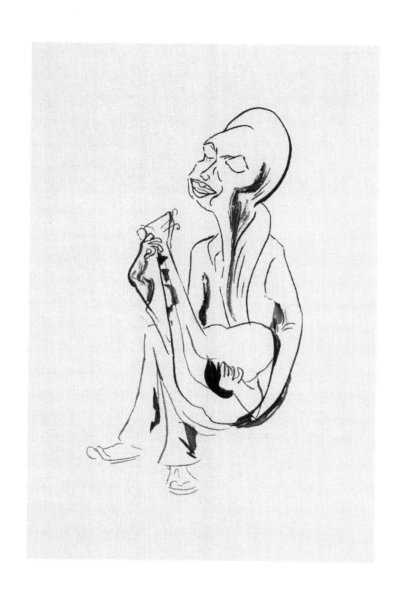

ACKNOWLEDGMENTS

Thanks to Sandy Ellston of Turnstone Books for her interest in including art with poetry, and for her patience in seeing the project through.

Thanks to my writing buddies and inspirations: The Allegores of California (Sandra Giedeman, David Ferrell, Jeanie Ardell, Orman Day, and Micaela Hanley Myers); Leah Maines of Finishing Line Press; and in Oregon the insightful and creative members of VoiceCatcher (especially Carolyn Martin, Toni Partington, Constance Hall, and Steve Williams), Women in Portland Publishing (especially Jen Weaver-Neist), and the poetry critique group in Scappoose (Barbara LaMorticella, Brittany Baldwin, Mary Slocum, and Leah Noble); the poets who enliven Open Poetry Mic in the Hillsboro Walters Cultural Arts Center (including Fred Melden, Rosemary Lombard, Joe Schrader, Gerlinde McDougall, Gary Kirby, Leslea Smith, and Ed Labadie), and Fred Melden and Rosemary Lombard who organize Conversations with Writers; all the forces for good in the Oregon Writers Colony (especially Marlene Howard, Rae Richen, Holly Franko, Cindy Brown, Judy Massee, Judy O'Neill, and Bill Cameron, a short list because there isn't enough space to name them all); Sandy Ellston of the Northwest Poets Concord; David Biespiel of the Attic Institute; Marie Buckley of the Oregon Poetry Association; Tony Pfannenstiel of *Faultlines*; Carter MacKenzie of Airlie Press; Paulann Petersen, Oregon's elegant Poet Laureate and tireless supporter of poets and poetry; Goody Cable and Sally Ford, who create the perfect ambience for writing in the Sylvia Beach Hotel; and the incomparable Brian Doyle whose *Mink River* captures Oregon's poetry of place.

The art in this book spans fifty years, from doodles of folk singers, snids, and confused philosophers done when I was sixteen to the travel journal sketches and masks (such as "Wolf Totem" on the cover) that are recent. I'm grateful for the support of fellow artists at the Oregon Society of Artists and the Oregon Watercolor Society (especially Rene Eisenbart, Linda Nye, Sharon King, Peggy Lindquist, Marcia Lynch, Janet Parker, Verna Pooler, Harriet Reiss, Laura Shea, and Connie Yost), but especially for a public education that considered art to be central, not peripheral, to a well-educated citizen (thank you, Mark Wilensky and Richard Ness, Highland High School, Albuquerque, New Mexico).

And finally, thanks to my daughter, Gigi Pandian, fellow writer and my favorite traveling companion, whose battle with breast cancer inspired much of the angst and joy of this book, and to her father, my beloved J.

Made in the USA
San Bernardino, CA
29 November 2014